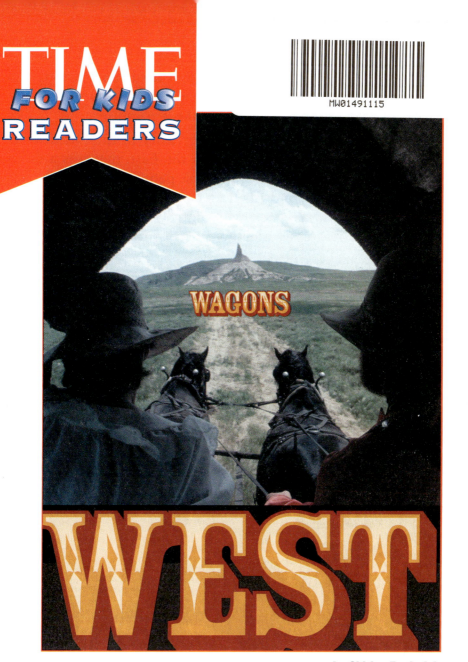

WAGONS

WEST

by Shirley Frederick

Harcourt

Orlando   Austin   Chicago   New York   Toronto   London   San Diego

Visit *The Learning Site!*
www.harcourtschool.com

In the 1830s, Americans were going through hard times. Crops failed. Banks closed. Workers lost their jobs. People told stories about a place called Oregon. They made it sound like a paradise.

Oregon was not a state then. It was a territory in the Northwest. To Americans living in the Midwest and in the East, that was a faraway place. Other than Native Americans, the first people to go to Oregon were explorers, fur trappers, and fur traders. Their stories told of a place with rich farmland, tall trees, wild animals for food, and good weather. Living there was easy, said those early adventurers.

Oregon was not yet part of the United States, but it held the promise of a better life. So thousands of people—from Massachusetts, Arkansas, Missouri, Kentucky, Illinois, New York, Iowa, and Indiana—gave up their homes, said goodbye to their families, and headed west. Because they were leaving their homeland these people were called emigrants.

Pioneers cross the plains near the Rocky Mountains.

OREGON COUNTRY

MICHIGAN TERRITORY

Unorganized Territory

(Mexico)

MISSOURI (1821)

ARKANSAS TERRITORY (1828)

FLORIDA TERRITORY (1822)

The red line shows the route to Oregon. This route is called the Oregon Trail.

Groups of travelers were usually made up of relatives or people from the same hometown. In some cases they formed companies, such as the Wild Rovers or the Peoria Pioneers. The size of the wagon trains varied. One group started out with 143 men, 3 women, 2 boys, 72 wagons, 93 horses, 66 oxen, 52 mules, 19 cows, 17 dogs, and some chickens.

Leaving home was not easy. Emigrants knew that when they moved far away, they might never again see their friends and families. Some pioneers had their photographs taken so the people left behind would remember them.

"I have been thinking of my beloved parents this evening, of the parting scene, of the probability that I shall never see those dear faces again while I live," wrote Narcissa Whitman in her journal in 1836.

The journey west was long and difficult. Good planning before leaving was important. Emigrants had to decide what to take and how to take it. Strong wagons were built just for the trip. Goods were arranged carefully so they would stay clean and dry. Dishes were packed in cornmeal or straw so they wouldn't break. Men and boys wore long-sleeved shirts and long pants, boots, and a hat with a wide brim for protection from the sun. Women and girls wore long dresses and bonnets.

Many emigrants used animals to help them carry all the things they needed. Oxen are strong and reliable but slow. It cost less to feed oxen than horses. Mules are faster than oxen but are stubborn. Horses are big and can carry a person across a deep river, but they eat a lot. Emigrants had to decide which animals to take.

Sturdy wagons had large wooden wheels with iron rims.

What Pioneers Took with Them

- flour
- sugar
- lard
- bacon
- dried fruit
- salt
- coffee and tea
- pots and pans
- plates and cups
- matches
- soap
- blankets
- pillows
- feather beds
- towels
- toothbrushes
- clothing
- candles
- tents
- lanterns
- needles and thread
- paper and pens
- family photos
- medicine
- rope
- tools
- knives
- guns
- gunpowder
- plants and seeds

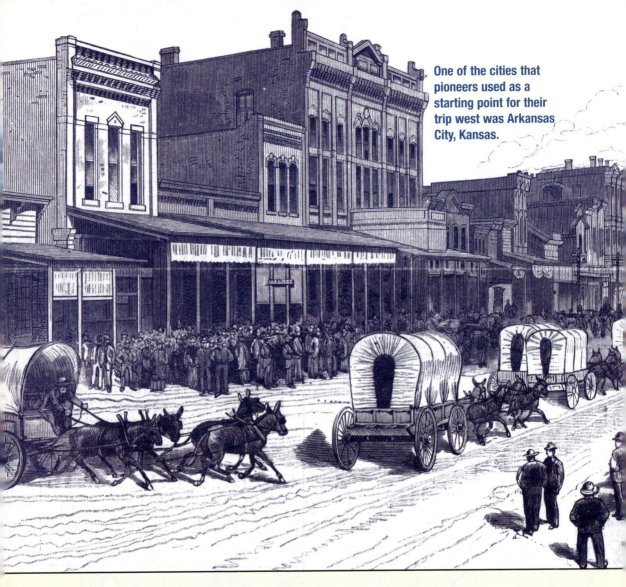

One of the cities that pioneers used as a starting point for their trip west was Arkansas City, Kansas.

Independence, Missouri, was a popular place to start the journey west. It is near the Missouri River so travelers could get there by boat. Emigrants gathered in Independence, got to know one another, and formed wagon trains. The travelers bought supplies. Blacksmiths made metal shoes for the horses, oxen, and mules. These shoes would protect the animals' hooves on the rocky trail ahead.

Independence, Missouri, was also a place where emigrants could get information about the trip. How can I find a guide? Where is the good water on the route? Is there enough grass to feed my animals? Most people left Independence in April, when the grass had started to grow. That gave them time to finish their journey before winter storms set in.

The route these pioneers took is called the Oregon Trail. It wasn't one single, neat trail, but a web of paths that were often rocky and muddy. Travelers followed the Platte River across the prairie and crossed the Rocky Mountains at South Pass. From there they followed the Snake River and then the Columbia River to Oregon. The trail is 2,170 miles (3,492 km) long, and the trip took five months. Often there was a fork in the trail, and travelers had to make choices. Gold seekers traveled partway on the Oregon Trail and then headed on the California Trail to the gold fields.

Since people and livestock needed water all along the way, most of the Oregon Trail followed rivers. There were a few stretches with no water. These were sometimes crossed at night when the temperatures were cooler and less water was needed by thirsty people and animals.

People loaded up their wagons with supplies before the long trek began.

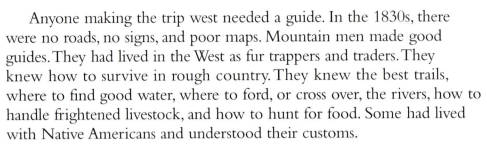

Anyone making the trip west needed a guide. In the 1830s, there were no roads, no signs, and poor maps. Mountain men made good guides. They had lived in the West as fur trappers and traders. They knew how to survive in rough country. They knew the best trails, where to find good water, where to ford, or cross over, the rivers, how to handle frightened livestock, and how to hunt for food. Some had lived with Native Americans and understood their customs.

Emigrants traveling together elected a captain. Still, there were disagreements. Who would go first? How fast should they travel? Where should they camp? Some people couldn't agree. In that case, some decided to leave the wagon train to make it on their own.

Mountain men knew the paths west and guided emigrants over them.

TFK FAST FACTS

Among the Pioneers

Missionaries are people who teach their religion to others. Often they travel far and endure hardships. In the 1830s, missionaries wanted to bring their religion to the American Indians. To do this, they traveled west and set up missions in Oregon.

Mormons were one type of missionary. Their religion had customs far different from those of most pioneers from the East. As a result, Mormons were not popular in the 1800s. After their leader, Joseph Smith, was killed, the Mormons decided to head west. They left their homes in Nauvoo, Illinois, in 1846. They went far west and settled in Utah. There they hoped to live in peace. Today, Utah still has a large Mormon population.

Pioneers added to their diet by hunting along the trail.

On the trail, the day began early. Narcissa Whitman wrote, "In the morning as soon as the day breaks the first that we hear is the words, Arise! Arise! Then the mules set up a noise as you never heard, which puts the whole camp in motion."

The animals had spent the night grazing and had to be rounded up. The women got the children up, cooked breakfast, washed the dishes, and packed up the wagons. The men hitched the animals to the wagons. When everyone was ready, a signal was given. "Wagons ho!" The wagons started to roll. They were heavily loaded and they bumped along slowly over the uneven ground. Most people walked.

Mary Ellen Murdock Compton, one pioneer, started from Independence with 10 new pairs of shoes. She wore out all of them except the last pair. She saved this pair for the Oregon Country by walking barefoot over the last miles of her journey.

When large numbers of people and livestock traveled together, dust was a big problem. The wagons spread out across the prairie, instead of traveling single file. Still, the people at the back of the wagon train got the worst of it.

Many emigrants soon found that their wagons were too heavy. Then they had to make decisions. What was needed for the trip and what was not? The Oregon Trail became a trail of precious belongings left behind. One traveler wrote that he could have set up a furniture store with the things he found on a 10-mile (17-km) stretch of trail. Women like Narcissa Whitman sadly said goodbye to family treasures.

Along the way, she sent a letter to a friend back home. "Dear Harriet," she wrote, "the little trunk you gave me has come with me so far. Now I must leave it here alone. Poor little trunk, I am sorry to leave thee. . . . Below the falls on Snake River this shall be thy place of rest. Farewell, little trunk. . . ."

The emigrants wanted to travel as far as possible each day. On a good day they could go 20 miles (32 km). On an average day they went 15 miles (24 km). At the end of the day they camped. The leaders looked for good grass for the livestock and good water for drinking. Women prepared the evening meal and washed the dishes. By 9 P.M. everyone was in bed. Most people slept on the ground. They weren't comfortable, but they were tired enough to sleep. As they slept, a guard watched for signs of danger.

In some wagon trains, families took turns being at the front of the line so they could avoid the dust.

A noon break was called *nooning*. Both people and animals were glad to rest. Breakfast leftovers became the noon meal. Children played and women wrote letters. Men checked the animals and the wagons. James Coon reported in his journal that the wagons "laid by." He meant the wagons stopped by the side of the trail. "Set tires and shod some horses and oxen."

Sometimes the travelers even stopped for a day. At times the weather was bad. Wind, rain, and hail slowed progress. After a big thunderstorm, the water in the creeks rose. Then the travelers had to wait a day or two for the water to go down so they could cross.

In 1864, a man named William Lieuallen, who clearly was not a great speller, wrote: "Travel about 10 miles (17 km) and stopt to noon & it thundred & rained & hailed as hard as I ever seen . . . A little dry brook raised so we could not cross it. Campt on the river."

At other times, stops were made because chores needed to be done. Women washed and mended clothes. Men fixed the wagons and took care of the livestock.

On one Saturday, Narcissa Whitman wrote: "Last night I put my clothes in water and this morning finished washing before breakfast. This is the third time I have washed since I left home."

A special modern-day tour allows people to see what life was like for pioneers on the Oregon Trail. With the wagon train parked near Bayard, Nebraska, a woman cooks at a chuck wagon.

Words of the West

anvil a heavy tool used to work with metal

chuck wagon the wagon in which food was prepared and cooked

creek small river

emigrant a person who leaves one place to live in another

ferry a raft that transports people and goods across a river

ford a shallow place in a river; to wade across a river, or drive a wagon across

lard animal fat

livestock horses, mules, and cattle

mission a place where missionaries taught their religion to others

mountain men fur trappers who lived in the West before it was settled

nooning resting at noon

ox yoke a wooden frame put around the necks of oxen

oxen cattle used to do work

pass a place where a mountain range can be crossed

portage carrying wagons, boats, and supplies around rapids or waterfalls

rapids river water flowing fast over rocks

shod to put new shoes on an animal

toll money charged for the use of a ferry or a road

About one out of five women were expecting babies while on the Oregon Trail.

Life went on in many ways. Along the trail, babies were born. When it was time for a mother to give birth, the other women helped. If a woman was sick or weak, another woman took care of her baby. Some families adopted children whose parents had died.

More and more emigrants headed west. As they traveled they changed the environment. Their livestock ate the grass along the way. Travelers hunted wildlife and burned firewood.

Emigrants became ill because of diseases such as measles, smallpox, and cholera (KAWL•er•uh). Most of the people who died on the way west died of disease. Cholera was the most serious. Those who died from it were buried quickly so the disease would not spread. Mountain fever was spread by ticks, tiny insects that bite. Insects were annoying and a problem for both people and animals. Narcissa Whitman wrote: "I put my hand under my cape and took from thence two insects, which I soon discovered to be fleas. Immediately I cast my eyes upon my dress . . . and, to my astonishment, found it was black with these creatures, making all possible speed to lay siege to my neck and ears."

The pioneers ate whatever they could hunt or scrounge. They ate deer, buffalo, elk, prairie dogs, antelope, catfish, trout, and quail. They sometimes managed to make hardtack, a hard bread made from flour and water, and pancakes made from flour, water, baking soda, and salt. Johnnycakes were a treat. They were made from cornmeal, water, and baking soda and baked in a Dutch oven, a heavy cast-iron pot with a cast-iron lid that sat in the coals of a fire.

TFK FAST FACTS

A Helping Hand

The emigrants traveled through Indian country. Native Americans had lived on these lands for hundreds of years. At first, the Indians thought the emigrants were just passing through and often helped them. They found lost animals. They rescued drowning people. They pulled wagons out of the mud. They traded horses for clothing and food for guns. Some asked for payment for crossing their lands.

James Coon mentions this in his diary. "Camped at a Sioux Indian town. Quite a trade was got up by the women . . . trading beads and other trinkets for bread and meat. At Fort Laramie the old Chief told us we had to pay him for passing through his country. The commander at the Post told us it was customary to give him something. [The Chief] spread down his blanket and each man put on his pay, some flour, some meat, coffee, beans, peas, dried fruit, etc. He was well pleased."

Often the water was either muddy or tasted bad. So it was boiled to kill any germs it might contain. Pioneers with milk cows had milk, cream, and butter. Sometimes, though, the diet was neither healthful nor tasty. One traveler, Samuel Parker, recorded in 1836 that "dry bread and bacon consisted our breakfast, dinner, and supper. The bacon we cooked when we could obtain wood for fire. But when nothing but green grass could be seen, we ate our bacon without cooking."

From 1841 to 1861, about 300,000 people followed the Oregon Trail.

Travelers who ate nothing but bread and bacon suffered from scurvy. Scurvy is caused by a lack of vitamin C, which is mainly found in fruit. Tea made from green pine needles or berries of the wild rose was a source of vitamin C.

Graves along the way told a tale of hardship and sadness. But one of James Coon's journal entries from 1847 shows there was little time for being sad. "Buried Turner's son, three years old. Left south fork of the Platt at 12 o'clock."

The diseases that struck the travelers also caused terrible suffering and much death among the Native American tribes. Never having experienced these illnesses, they had built up no resistance. Life for the Native Americans became very difficult.

As more and more pioneers entered Indian territory tensions grew. The United States Congress voted to build forts along the Oregon Trail. A fur trading company built Fort Laramie in Wyoming. In 1849, the United States Army bought the fort and sent in soldiers to protect the trail. Fort Laramie and other forts were good places for weary travelers to stop and rest and stock up on food. But the presence of soldiers was not good news for the Native Americans.

When Buffalo Roamed

Emigrants crossing the prairie saw large herds of buffalo. "Buffalo extended the whole length of our afternoon's travel . . . I estimated two million," wrote traveler William Kilgore. The buffalo were hunted for food. Their droppings were round and flat and about as big as a plate. When fresh they were wet and gooey, but in the hot sun they soon dried out. They were called buffalo chips. On the prairie there was little firewood, and buffalo chips were used as cooking fuel. Dried buffalo chips burned well and gave off no odor. As time went on and the trail grew more crowded, cooks competed for the biggest, driest chips. Children helped collect them and discovered they made good toys to toss—pioneer Frisbees!

Buffalo provided food—and fuel.

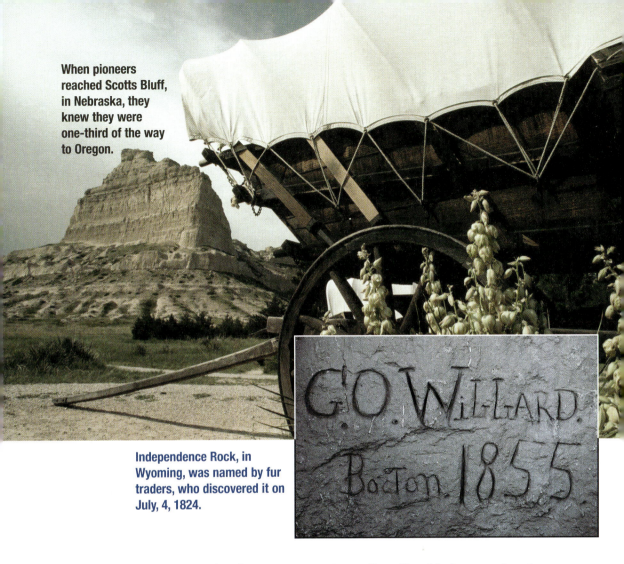

When pioneers reached Scotts Bluff, in Nebraska, they knew they were one-third of the way to Oregon.

Independence Rock, in Wyoming, was named by fur traders, who discovered it on July, 4, 1824.

Landmarks in the distance, sometimes far off, told the travelers how far they had come. The landmarks on the Oregon Trail were usually rocks with unusual shapes. One of the first was Chimney Rock in Nebraska. It could be seen from up to 40 miles (64 km) away. The travelers rarely stopped to admire the landscape. They were eager to move on. Still, they saw natural beauty everywhere. Soon after Chimney Rock, they could see Scotts Bluff. This was a great mound of rock that rose up out of the prairie grasses.

Travelers wanted to reach Independence Rock by the Fourth of July. Then they knew they were traveling fast enough to reach Oregon by September. Independence Rock was a place to stop and rest. Thousands of names were carved on the rock by people who stopped there.

The West has wide rivers with fast-moving water. As the wagon trains bumped over the rough trail, they also had to make it across those rivers. There were no bridges. Some rivers had fords, shallow places where people and animals could wade across. Sometimes there were ferries. These were rafts used to carry wagons and people. To use a ferry, travelers had to pay a toll. The ferry toll was about $16, which was more than many groups could afford. One ferry earned $65,000 in one year—a fortune in those days.

Ferries sometimes carried wagons across a river. A rope tied to the boat and to trees on opposite banks kept the boat from drifting downriver.

A watertight wagon box—the part of the wagon that held the cargo—could be floated across a river. In some places, simple boats carried passengers and goods across.

River crossings were one of the most dangerous parts of the trail. People and animals sometimes lost their lives. Thirty-seven people drowned in 1850 trying to cross the Green River in Wyoming.

If the water was deep, livestock had to swim. Caught in a swift current, some animals panicked. The men worked hard to keep the herd under control. "We were all day swimming our cattle across. Two or three were killed and three or four crippled," wrote James Coon. "It's a very rocky ford and the water runs very rapidly."

Covered wagons were not built for crossing mountain passes. Going up a pass was hard enough. Coming down the other side was even harder. Brakes on the wagons sometimes gave out, and then the oxen could not hold the wagons back.

Narcissa Whitman recorded her impressions: "Before noon we began to descend one of the most terrible mountains for steepness and length I have yet seen. . . . The horses appeared to dread the hill as much as I did. They would turn and wind around in a zigzag manner all the way down."

For the last part of the journey, people traveled by boat or raft down the Columbia River. The Dalles was an especially dangerous part of the river. Water flowed rapidly between walls of rock. Some travelers took the risk of running the rapids in their boats.

Others chose to portage, or to carry, their boats and goods around the rapids. In 1845 the Barlow Toll Road opened. It was named for Sam Barlow, who helped the first wagon train along that route. It was a much safer way to Oregon, but travelers had to pay to use it. In 1846, the road tolls were $5 for each wagon and 10 cents for every head of livestock. This was at a time when people earned an average of $5 a week.

"We came to the Dalles just before noon," Narcissa Whitman wrote. "Here our boat was stopped by two rocks of immense size and height, all

the water of the river passing between them in a narrow channel, and with great rapidity. Here we were obliged to land and make a portage of two and a half miles, carrying the boat also."

After four to six months of hardship, emigrants reached the end of the trail. Some sighed with relief. Some celebrated. Some joined family members who were already there. All were thankful that they had survived. They didn't rest for long, though. They built houses, cleared fields, and taught school lessons to the children. More people came. Towns grew. Before long, Oregon began to look very much like the places emigrants had left behind.

Hiram Larkin, an emigrant, wrote: "I am thankful that we have at last reached Oregon. The land is better than we had hoped, and our prospects are bright."

When the pioneers reached Oregon, they were tired—and thankful.

Over many years, wagon wheels wore these ruts into sandstone on the Oregon Trail in Wyoming.

The Oregon Trail Today

Today people who are interested in history can still follow the Oregon Trail. In 150 years much has changed. Independence, once a small frontier town, is now a busy city. Cars and trucks travel at 60 miles (more than 96 km) an hour. Bridges take the place of fords and ferries. Towns and cities have grown along rivers and highways. Telephone and power lines carry electricity across the landscape.

Yet some things haven't changed. Scotts Bluff and Chimney and Independence Rocks still watch over the trail. The travelers along the Oregon Trail are not forgotten. They not only left us their journals, but also their photographs and their names carved in rock. Their wagon wheels made ruts that rain and wind have not erased. Fort Laramie, South Pass, and other sites along the trail have been preserved. The story of the pioneers is an important part of the story of our nation.